The Mind Of Money: The Blueprint of Accumulating Wealth

By
Justin Perry, Wallace D Wattles, Joseph Murphy, Henry Harrison Brown, & Florence Scovel Shinn

YouAreCreators

P.O. Box 756

Tinley Park, IL 60477

Table of Contents

The secrets of obtaining wealth and financial security has long been a topic among men and women throughout the centuries. How does one become wealthy? What are the steps to financial security? Why do some people seem to obtain riches easily while others remain in a constant state of struggle? The contents in this book clearly answers these questions and contains the formula to obtaining wealth on a master scale. I myself have used the wisdom within this book and have become financially independent, creating a multiple 6 figure income working from home. Trust me, this information works and will always work! This is what you call "Timeless Knowledge". In a thousand years, this knowledge will still prove to be accurate and true. I am thrilled to present this book to you, for it is my passion and purpose to remind you of the true nature of abundance. I have collected and gathered the work of 4 "Mind Science" geniuses (Wallace D Wattles, Joseph Murphy, Henry Harrison Brown, Florence Scovel Shinn) and put them all in one small book! What you're about read is the clearest blueprint to forming the foundation of accumulating material wealth. The message is simple, the message is clear: You're supposed to be prosperous, you deserve to be rich, and wealth is your birthright. Enough with the small talk, let's learn the secrets to wealth.

Wallace D Wattles

WHATEVER may be said in praise of poverty, the fact remains that it is not possible to live a really complete or successful life unless one is rich. No man can rise to his greatest possible height in talent or soul development unless he has plenty of money; for to unfold the soul and to develop talent he must have many things to use, and he cannot have these things unless he has money to buy them with.

A man develops in mind, soul, and body by making use of things, and society is so organized that man must have money in order to become the possessor of things; therefore, the basis of all advancement for man must be the science of getting rich.

The object of all life is development; and everything that lives has an inalienable right to all the development it is capable of attaining. Man's right to life means his right to have the free and unrestricted use of all the things which may be necessary to his fullest mental, spiritual, and physical unfoldment; or, in other words, his right to be rich.

In this book, I shall not speak of riches in a figurative way; to be really rich does not mean to be satisfied or contented with a little. No man ought to be satisfied with a little if he is capable of using and enjoying more. The purpose of Nature is the advancement and unfoldment of life; and every man should have all that can contribute to the power; elegance, beauty, and richness of life; to be content with less is sinful.

The man who owns all he wants for the living of all the life he is capable of living is rich; and no man who has not plenty of money can have all he wants. Life has advanced so far, and become so complex, that even the most ordinary man or woman requires a great amount of wealth in order to live in a manner that even approaches completeness. Every person naturally wants to become all that they are capable of becoming; this desire to realize innate possibilities is inherent in human nature; we cannot help wanting to be all that we can be. Success in life is becoming what you want to be; you can become what you want to be only by making use of things, and you can have the free use of things only as you become rich enough to buy them. To understand the science of getting rich is therefore the most essential of all knowledge.

There is nothing wrong in wanting to get rich. The desire for riches is really the desire for a richer, fuller, and more abundant life; and that desire is praise worthy. The man who does not desire to live more abundantly is abnormal, and so the man who does not desire to have money enough to buy all he wants is abnormal. There are three motives for which we live; we live for the body, we live for the mind, we live for the soul. No one of these is better or holier than the other; all are alike desirable, and no one of the three—body, mind, or soul —

can live fully if either of the others is cut short of full life and expression. It is not right or noble to live only for the soul and deny mind or body; and it is wrong to live for the intellect and deny body or soul.

We are all acquainted with the loathsome consequences of living for the body and denying both mind and soul; and we see that real life means the complete expression of all that man can give forth through body, mind, and soul. Whatever he can say, no man can be really happy or satisfied unless his body is living fully in every function, and unless the same is true of his mind and his soul. Wherever there is unexpressed possibility, or function not performed, there is unsatisfied desire. Desire is possibility seeking expression, or function seeking performance.

Man cannot live fully in body without good food, comfortable clothing, and warm shelter; and without freedom from excessive toil. Rest and recreation are also necessary to his physical life.

He cannot live fully in mind without books and time to study them, without opportunity for travel and observation, or without intellectual companionship.

To live fully in mind he must have intellectual recreations, and must surround himself with all the objects of art and beauty he is capable of using and appreciating.

To live fully in soul, man must have love; and love is denied expression by poverty. A man's highest happiness is found in the bestowal of benefits on those he loves; love finds its most natural and spontaneous expression in giving. The man who has nothing to give cannot fill his place as a husband or father, as a citizen, or as a man. It is in the use of material things that a man finds full life for his body, develops his mind, and unfolds his soul. It is therefore of supreme importance to him that he should be rich.

It is perfectly right that you should desire to be rich; if you are a normal man or woman you cannot help doing so. It is perfectly right that you should give your best attention to the Science of Getting Rich, for it is the noblest and most necessary of all studies. If you neglect this study, you are derelict in your duty to yourself, to God and humanity; for you can render to God and humanity no greater service than to make the most of yourself.

There is a Science of getting rich, and it

is an exact science, like algebra or arithmetic. There are certain laws that govern the process of acquiring riches; once these laws are learned and obeyed by any man, he will get rich with mathematical certainty.

The ownership of money and property comes as a result of doing things in a certain way; those who do things in this Certain Way, whether on purpose or accidentally, get rich; while those who do not do things in this Certain Way, no matter how hard they work or how able they are, remain poor.

It is a natural law that like causes always produce like effects; and, therefore, any man or woman who learns to do things in this certain way will infallibly get rich. That the above statement is true is shown by the following facts:

Getting rich is not a matter of environment, for, if it were, all the people in certain neighborhoods would become wealthy; the people of one city would all be rich, while those of other towns would all be poor; or the inhabitants of one state would roll in wealth, while those of an adjoining state would be in poverty.

But everywhere we see rich and poor living side-by-side, in the same environment, and often engaged in the same vocations. When two men are in the same locality, and in the same business, and one gets rich while the other remains poor, it shows that getting rich is not, primarily, a matter of environment. Some environments may be more favorable than others, but when two men in the same business are in the same neighborhood, and one gets rich while the other fails, it indicates that getting rich is the result of doing things in a Certain Way. And further, the ability to do things in this certain way is not due solely to the possession of talent, for many people who have great talent remain poor, while other who have very little talent get rich.

Studying the people who have got rich, we find that they are an average lot in all respects, having no greater talents and abilities than other men. It is evident that they do not get rich because they possess talents and abilities that other men have not, but because they happen to do things in a Certain Way.

The Power of Thought

THOUGHT is the only power which can produce tangible riches from the Formless Substance. The stuff from which all things are made is a substance which thinks, and a thought of form in this substance produces the form.

Original Substance moves according to its thoughts; every form and process you see in nature is the visible expression of a thought in Original Substance. As the Formless Stuff thinks of a form, it takes that form; as it thinks of a motion, it makes that motion. That is the way all things were created. We live in a thought world, which is part of a thought universe. The thought of a moving universe extended throughout Formless Substance, and the Thinking Stuff moving according to that thought, took the form of systems of planets, and maintains that form. Thinking Substance takes the form of its thought, and moves according to the thought. Holding the idea of a circling system of suns and worlds, it takes the form of these bodies, and moves them as it thinks. Thinking the form of a slow-growing oak tree, it moves accordingly, and produces the tree, though centuries may be required to do the work. In creating, the Formless seems to move according to the lines of motion it has established; the thought of an oak tree does not cause the instant formation of a full-grown tree, but it does start in motion the forces which will produce the tree, along established lines of growth.

Every thought of form, held in thinking Substance, causes the creation of the form, but always, or at least generally, along lines of growth and action already established.

The thought of a house of a certain construction, if it were impressed upon

Formless Substance, might not cause the instant formation, of the house; but it would cause the turning of creative energies already working in trade and commerce into such channels as to result in the speedy building of the house. And if there were no existing channels through which the creative energy could work, then the house would be formed directly from primal substance, without waiting for the slow processes of the organic and inorganic world.

No thought of form can be impressed upon Original Substance without causing the creation of the form. Man is a thinking center, and can originate thought. All the forms that man fashions with his hands must first exist in his thought; he cannot shape a thing until he has thought that thing.

And so far man has confined his efforts wholly to the work of his hands; he has applied manual labor to the world of forms, seeking to change or modify those already existing. He has never thought of trying to cause the creation of new forms by impressing his thoughts upon Formless Substance.

When man has a thought-form, he takes material from the forms of nature, and makes an image of the form which is in his mind. He has, so far, made little or no effort to co-operate with Formless Intelligence; to work "with the Father." He has not dreamed that he can "do what he seeth the Father doing." Man reshapes and modifies existing forms by manual labor; he has given no attention to the question whether he may not produce things from Formless Substance by communicating his thoughts to it. We propose to prove that he may do so; to prove that any man or woman may do so, and to show how.

As our first step, we must lay down three fundamental propositions. First, we assert that there is one original formless stuff, or substance, from which all things are made. All the seemingly many elements are but different presentations of one element; all the many forms found in organic and inorganic nature are but different shapes, made from the same stuff. And this stuff is thinking stuff; a thought held in it produces the form of the thought. Thought, in thinking substance, produces shapes. Man is a thinking center, capable of original thought; if man can communicate his thought to original thinking substance, he can cause the creation, or formation, of the thing he thinks about. To summarize this:

There is a thinking stuff from which all things are made, and which, in its original state, permeates, penetrates, and fills the interspaces of the universe. A thought, in this substance, Produces the thing that is imaged by the thought.

Man can form things in his thought, and, by impressing his thought upon formless substance, can cause the thing he thinks about to be created. It may be asked if I can prove these statements; and without going into details, I answer that I can do so, both by logic and experience.

Reasoning back from the phenomena of form and thought, I come to one original thinking substance; and reasoning forward from this thinking substance, I come to man's power to cause the formation of the thing he thinks about.

And by experiment, I find the reasoning true; and this is my strongest proof. If one man who reads this book gets rich by doing what it tells him to do, that is evidence in support of my claim; but if every man who does what it tells him to do gets rich, that is positive proof until someone goes through the process and fails. The theory is true until the process fails; and this process will not fail, for every man who does exactly what this book tells him to do will get rich.

I have said that men get rich by doing things in a Certain Way; and in order to do so, men must become able to think in a certain way.

A man's way of doing things is the direct result of the way he thinks about things.

To do things in a way you want to do them, you will have to acquire the ability to think the way you want to think; this is the first step toward getting rich.

To think what you want to think is to think TRUTH, regardless of appearances.

Every man has the natural and inherent power to think what he wants to think, but it requires far more effort to do so than it does to think the thoughts which are suggested by appearances. To think according to appearance is easy; to think truth regardless of appearances is laborious, and requires the expenditure of more power than any other work man is called upon to perform.

There is no labor from which most people shrink as they do from that of sustained and consecutive thought; it is the hardest work in the world. This is especially true when truth is contrary to appearances. Every appearance in the visible world tends to produce a corresponding form in the mind which observes it; and this can only be prevented by holding the thought of the TRUTH.

To look upon the appearance of disease will produce the form of disease in your own mind, and ultimately in your body, unless you hold the thought of the truth, which is that there is no disease; it is only an appearance, and the reality is health.

To look upon the appearances of poverty will produce corresponding forms in your own mind, unless you hold to the truth that there is no poverty; there is only abundance.

To think health when surrounded by the appearances of disease, or to think riches when in the midst of appearances of poverty, requires power; but he who acquires this power becomes a MASTER MIND. He can conquer fate; he can have what he wants.

This power can only be acquired by getting hold of the basic fact which is behind all appearances; and that fact is that there is one Thinking Substance, from which and by which all things are made.

Then we must grasp the truth that every thought held in this substance becomes a form, and that man can so impress his thoughts upon it as to cause them to take form and become visible things.

When we realize this, we lose all doubt and fear, for we know that we can create what we want to create; we can get what we want to have, and can become what we want to be. As a first step toward getting rich, you must believe the three fundamental statements given previously in this chapter; and in order to emphasize them. I repeat them here:-

There is a thinking stuff from which all things are made, and which, in its original state, permeates, penetrates, and fills the interspaces of the universe. A thought, in this substance, Produces the thing that is imaged by the thought.

Man can form things in his thought, and, by impressing his thought upon formless substance, can cause the thing he thinks about to be created.

You must lay aside all other concepts of the universe than this monistic one; and you must dwell upon this until it is fixed in your mind, and has become your habitual thought.

Read these creed statements over and over again; fix every word upon your memory, and meditate upon them until you firmly believe what they say. If a doubt comes to you, cast it aside as a sin. Do not listen to arguments against this idea; do not go to churches or lectures where a contrary concept of things is taught or preached. Do not read magazines or books which teach a different idea; if you get mixed up in your faith, all your efforts will be in vain.

Do not ask why these things are true, nor speculate as to how they can be true; simply take them on trust. The science of getting rich begins with the absolute acceptance of this Faith.

There is a thinking stuff from which all things are made, and which, in its original state, permeates, penetrates, and fills the interspaces of the universe. A thought, in this substance, produces the thing that is imaged by the thought.

Man can form things in his thought, and, by impressing his thought upon formless substance, can cause the thing he thinks about to be created. In order to do this, man must pass from the competitive to the creative mind; he must form a clear mental picture of the things he wants, and hold this picture in his thoughts with the fixed PURPOSE to get what he wants, and the unwavering FAITH that he does get what he wants, closing his mind against all that may tend to shake his purpose, dim his vision, or quench his faith.

And in addition to all this, we shall now see that he must live and act in a Certain Way.

ACTING IN THE CERTAIN WAY

THOUGHT is the creative power, or the impelling force which causes the creative power to act; thinking in a Certain Way will bring riches to you, but you must not rely upon thought alone, paying no attention to personal action. That is the rock upon which many otherwise scientific metaphysical thinkers meet shipwreck—the failure to connect thought with personal action. We have not yet reached the stage of development, even supposing such a stage to be possible, in which man can create directly from Formless Substance without nature's processes or the work of human hands; man must not only think, but his personal action must supplement his thought.

By thought you can cause the gold in the hearts of the mountains to be impelled toward you; but it will not mine itself, refine itself, coin itself into double eagles, and come rolling along the roads seeking its way into your pocket.

Under the impelling power of the Supreme Spirit, men's affairs will be so ordered that someone will be led to mine the gold for you; other men's business transactions will be so directed that the gold will be brought toward you, and you must so arrange your own business affairs that you may be able to receive it when it comes to you. Your thought makes all things, animate and inanimate, work to bring you what you want; but your personal activity must be such that you can rightly receive what you want when it reaches you. You are not to take it as charity, nor to steal it; you must give every man more in use value than he gives you in cash value. The scientific use of thought consists in forming a clear and distinct mental image of what you want; in holding fast to the purpose to get what you want; and in realizing with grateful faith that you do get what you want.

Do not try to project your thought in any mysterious or occult way, with the idea of having it go and do things for you; that is wasted effort, and will weaken your power to think with sanity.

The action of thought in getting rich is fully explained in the preceding chapters; your faith and purpose positively impress your vision upon Formless Substance, which has THE SAME DESIRE FOR MORE LIFE THAT YOU HAVE; and this vision, received from you, sets all the creative forces at work IN AND THROUGH

THEIR REGULAR CHANNELS OF ACTION, but directed toward you.

It is not your part to guide or supervise the creative process; all you have to do with that is to retain your vision, stick to your purpose, and maintain your faith and gratitude.

Joseph Murphy

If you are having financial difficulties, if you are trying to make ends meet, it means you have not convinced your subconscious mind that you will always have plenty and some to spare. You know men and women who work a few hours a week and make fabulous sums of money. They do not strive or slave hard. Do not believe the story that the only way you can become wealthy is by the sweat of your brow and hard labor. It is not so; the effortless way of life is the best. Do the thing you love to do, and do it for the joy and thrill of it. I know an executive in Los Angeles who receives a salary of $75,000 yearly. Last year he went on a nine-month cruise seeing the world and its beauty spots. He said to me that he had succeeded in convincing his subconscious mind that he is worth that much money. He told me that many men in his organization getting about one hundred dollars a week knew more about the business than he did, and could manage it better, but they had no ambition, no creative ideas, and were not interested in the wonders of their subconscious mind.

Wealth is of the mind- Wealth is simply a subconscious conviction on the part of the individual. You can become a millionaire by saying, "I am a millionaire, I am a millionaire." (but it is rare) You will grow into a wealth consciousness by building into your mentality the idea of wealth and abundance.

Your invisible means of support- The trouble with most people is that they have no invisible means of support. When business falls away, the stock market drops, or they lose their investments, they seem helpless. The reason for such insecurity is that they do not know how to tap the subconscious mind. They are unacquainted with the inexhaustible storehouse within. A man with a poverty type mind finds himself in poverty stricken conditions.

Another man with a mind filled with ideas of wealth is surrounded with everything he needs. It was never intended that man should lead a life of indigence. You can have wealth, everything you need, and plenty to spare. Your words have power to cleanse your mind of wrong ideas and to instill right ideas in their place.

The ideal method for building a wealth consciousness- Perhaps you are saying as you read this chapter, "I need wealth and success." This is what you do: Repeat for about five minutes to yourself three or four times a day, "Wealth—Success." These words have tremendous power. They represent the inner power of the subconscious mind. Anchor your mind on this substantial power within you; then conditions and circumstances corresponding to their nature and quality will be manifested in your life. You are not saying, "I am wealthy," you are dwelling on real powers within you. There is no conflict in the mind when you say, "Wealth." Furthermore, the feeling of wealth will well up within you as you dwell on the idea of wealth. The feeling of wealth produces wealth; keep this in mind at all times. Your subconscious mind is like a bank, a sort of universal financial institution. It magnifies whatever you deposit or impress upon it whether it is the idea of wealth or of poverty. Choose wealth.

Why your affirmations for wealth fail- I have talked to many people during the past thirty-five years whose usual complaint is, "I have said for weeks and months, 'I am wealthy, I am prosperous,' and nothing has happened." I discovered that when they said, "I am prosperous, I am wealthy," they sometimes felt that they were lying to themselves. One man told me, "I have affirmed that I am prosperous until I am tired. Things are now worse. I knew when I made the statement that it was obviously not true." His statements were rejected by the conscious mind, and the very opposite of what he outwardly affirmed and claimed was made manifest. Your affirmation succeeds best when it is specific and when it does not produce a mental conflict or argument; hence the statements made by this man made matters worse because they suggested his lack. Your subconscious accepts what you really feel to be true, not just idle words or statements. The dominant idea or belief is always accepted by the subconscious mind.

How to avoid mental conflict- The following is the ideal way to overcome this conflict for those who have this difficulty. Make this practical statement frequently, particularly prior to sleep: "By day and by night I am being prospered in all of my interests." This affirmation will not arouse any argument because it does not contradict your subconscious mind's impression of financial lack. I suggested to one businessman whose sales and finances were very low and who was greatly worried, that he sit down in his office, become quiet, and repeat this statement over and over again: "My sales are improving every day." This statement engaged the co-operation of the conscious and subconscious mind; results followed.

Don't sign blank checks- You sign blank checks when you make such statements as, "There is not enough to go around." "There is a shortage." "I will lose the house because of the mortgage," etc. If you are full of fear about the future, you are also writing a blank check and attracting negative conditions to you. Your subconscious mind takes your fear and negative statement as your request and proceeds in its own way to bring obstacles, delays, lack, and limitation into your life.

Your subconscious gives you compound interest- To him that hath the feeling of wealth, more wealth shall be added; to him that hath the feeling of lack, more lack shall be added. Your subconscious multiplies and magnifies whatever you deposit in it. Every morning as you awaken deposit thoughts of prosperity, success, wealth, and peace. Dwell upon these concepts. Busy your mind with them as often as possible. These constructive thoughts will find their way as deposits in your subconscious mind, and bring forth abundance and prosperity.

Why nothing happened- I can hear you saying, "Oh, I did that and nothing happened." You did not get results because you indulged in fear thoughts perhaps ten minutes later and neutralized the good you had affirmed. When you place a seed in the ground, you do not dig it up. You let it take root and grow. Suppose, for example, you are going to say, "I shall not be able to make that payment." Before you get further than, "I shall—" stop the sentence and dwell on a constructive statement, such as, "By day and by night I am prospered in all my ways."

True source of wealth- Your subconscious mind is never short of ideas. There are within it an infinite number of ideas ready to flow into your conscious mind and appear as cash in your pocketbook in countless ways. This process will continue to go on in your mind regardless of whether the stock market goes up or down, or whether the pound sterling or dollar drops in value. Your wealth is never truly dependent on bonds, stocks, or money in the bank; these are really only symbols necessary and useful, of course, but only symbols. The point I wish to emphasize is that if you convince your subconscious mind that wealth is yours, and that it is always circulating in your life, you will always and inevitably have it, regardless of the form it takes.

Trying to make ends meet and the real cause- There are people who claim that they are always trying to make ends meet. They seem to have a great struggle to meet their obligations. Have you listened to their conversation? In many instances their conversation runs along this vein. They are constantly condemning those who have succeeded in life and who have raised their heads above the crowd. Perhaps they are saying, "Oh, that fellow has a racket; he is ruthless; he is a crook." This is why they lack; they are condemning the thing they desire and want. The reason they speak critically of their more prosperous associates is because they are envious and covetous of the others prosperity. The quickest way to cause wealth to take wings and fly away is to criticize and condemn others who have more wealth than you.

A common stumbling block to wealth
There is one emotion, which is the cause of the lack of wealth in the lives of many. Most people learn this the hard way. It is envy. For example, if you see a competitor depositing large sums of

money in the bank, and you have only a meager amount to deposit, does it make you envious? The way to overcome this emotion is to say to yourself, "Isn't it wonderful! I rejoice in that man's prosperity. I wish for him greater and greater wealth." To entertain envious thoughts is devastating because it places you in a very negative position; therefore, wealth flows from you instead of to you. If you are ever annoyed or irritated by the prosperity or great wealth of another, claim immediately that you truly wish for him greater wealth in every possible way. This will neutralize the negative thoughts in your mind and cause an ever-greater measure of wealth to flow to you by the law of your own subconscious mind.

Rubbing out a great mental block to wealth- If you are worried and critical about someone whom you claim is making money dishonestly, cease worrying about him. You know such a person is using the law of mind negatively; the law of mind takes care of him. Be careful not to criticize him for the reasons previously indicated. Remember: The block or obstacle to wealth is in your own mind. You can now destroy that mental block. This you may do by getting on mental good terms with everyone.

Sleep and grow rich- As you go to sleep at night, practice the following technique. Repeat the word, "Wealth," quietly, easily, and feelingly. Do this over and over again, just like a lullaby. Lull yourself to sleep with the one word, "Wealth." You should be amazed at the result. Wealth should flow to you in avalanches of abundance. This is another example of the magic power of your subconscious mind. Serve yourself with the powers of your mind

Decide to be wealthy the easy way, with the infallible aid of your subconscious mind.

Trying to accumulate wealth by the sweat of your brow and hard labor is one way to become the richest man in the graveyard. You do not have to strive or slave hard.

Wealth is a subconscious conviction. Build into your mentality the idea of wealth.

The trouble with most people is that they have no invisible means of support.

Repeat the word, "Wealth," to yourself slowly and quietly for about five minutes prior to sleep and your subconscious will bring wealth to pass in your experience.

The feeling of wealth produces wealth. Keep this in mind at all times.

Your subconscious accepts what you really feel to be true. The dominant idea is always accepted by your subconscious mind. The dominant idea should be wealth, not poverty.

You can overcome any mental conflict regarding wealth by affirming frequently, "By day and by night I am being prospered in all of my interests."

Increase your sales by repeating this statement over and over again, "My sales are improving every day; I am advancing, progressing, and getting wealthier every day."

Stop writing blank checks, such as, "There is not enough to go around," or "There is a shortage," etc. Such statements magnify and multiply your loss.

Deposit thoughts of prosperity, wealth, and success in your subconscious mind, and the latter will give you compound interest.

What you consciously affirm, you must not mentally deny a few moments later. This will neutralize the good you have affirmed.

Your true source of wealth consists of the ideas in your mind. You can have an idea worth millions of dollars. Your subconscious will give you the idea you seek.

Envy and jealousy are stumbling blocks to the flow of wealth. Rejoice in the prosperity of others.

The block to wealth is in your own mind. Destroy that block now by getting on good mental terms with everyone. It is your right to be rich. You are here to lead the abundant life and be happy, radiant, and free. You should, therefore, have all the money you need to lead a full, happy, and prosperous life. You are here to grow, expand, and unfold spiritually, mentally, and materially. You have the inalienable right to fully develop and express yourself along all lines. You should surround yourself with beauty and luxury. Why be satisfied with just enough to go around when you can enjoy the riches of your subconscious mind? In this chapter you can learn to make friends with money, and you should always have a surplus. Your desire to be rich is a desire for a fuller, happier, more wonderful life. It is a cosmic urge. It is not only good, but also very good.

Money is a symbol- Money is a symbol of exchange. It means to you not only freedom from want, but beauty, luxury, abundance, and refinement. It is merely a symbol of the economic health of the nation. When your blood is circulating freely in your body, you are healthy. When money is circulating freely in your life, you are economically healthy. When people begin to hoard money, to put it away in tin boxes, and become charged with fear, there is economic illness. Money has taken many forms as a medium of exchange down through the centuries, such as, salt, beads, and trinkets of various kinds. In early times a man's wealth was determined by the number of sheep and oxen he had. Now we use currency, and other negotiable instruments, as it is much more convenient to write a check than carry some sheep around with you to pay bills.

How to walk- The royal road to riches Knowledge of the powers of your subconscious mind is the means to the royal road to riches of all kinds—spiritual, mental, or financial. The student of the laws of mind believes and knows definitely that regardless of economic situations, stock market fluctuation, depression, strikes, war, other conditions or circumstances, he will always be amply supplied, regardless of what form money takes. The reason for this is that he has conveyed the idea of wealth to his subconscious mind, and it keeps him supplied wherever he may be. He has convinced himself in his mind that money is forever flowing freely in his life and that there is always a wonderful surplus. Should there be a financial collapse of government tomorrow and all the man's present holdings become valueless, as the German marks did after the First World War, he would still attract wealth and be cared for, regardless of the form the new currency took.

Why you do not have more money- As you read this chapter, you are probably saying, "I am worthy of a higher salary than I am receiving." I believe most people are inadequately compensated. One of the causes many people does not have more money is that they are silently or openly condemning it. They refer to money as "filthy lucre" or "the love of money is the root of all evil." Another reason they do not prosper is that they have a sneaky subconscious feeling there is some virtue in poverty. This subconscious pattern may be due to early childhood training, superstition, or it could be based on a false interpretation of scriptures.

Money and a balanced life- One time a man said to me, "I am broke. I do not like money. It is the root of all evil." These statements represent a confused neurotic mind. Love of money to the exclusion of everything else will cause you to become lopsided and unbalanced. You are here to use your power or authority wisely. Some men crave power others crave money. If you set your heart on money exclusively and say, "Money is all I want; I am going to give all my attention to amassing money; nothing else matters," you can get money and attain a fortune, but you have forgotten that you are here to lead a balanced life. You must also satisfy the hunger for peace of mind, harmony, love, joy, and perfect health. By making money your sole aim, you simply made a wrong choice. You thought that was all you wanted, but you found after all your efforts that it was not only the money you needed. You also desired true expression of your hidden talents, true place in life, beauty, and the joy of contributing to the welfare and success of others. By learning the laws of your subconscious mind, you could have a million dollars or many millions, if you wanted them, and still have peace of mind, harmony, perfect health, and perfect expression.

Poverty is a mental disease- There is no virtue in poverty; it is a disease like any other mental disease. If you were physically ill, you would think there was something wrong with you. You would seek help and do something about the condition at once. Likewise, if you do not have money constantly circulating in your life, there is something radically wrong with you. The urge of the life principle in you is toward growth, expansion, and the life more abundant. You are not here to live in a hovel, dress in rags, and go hungry. You should be happy, prosperous, and successful.

Why you must never criticize money-
Cleanse your mind of all weird and
superstitious beliefs about money. Do
not ever regard money as evil or filthy.
If you do, you cause it to take wings and
fly away from you. Remember that you
lose what you condemn. You cannot
attract what you criticize.

**Getting the right attitude toward
money-** Here is a simple technique you
may use to multiply money in your
experience. Use the following
statements several times a day, "I like
money, I love it, I use it wisely,
constructively, and judiciously. Money

is constantly circulating in my life. I release it with joy, and it returns to me multiplied in a wonderful way. It is good and very good. Money flows to me in avalanches of abundance. I use it for good only, and I am grateful for my good and for the riches of my mind."

How the scientific thinker looks at money- Suppose, for example, you found gold, silver, lead, copper, or iron in the ground. Would you pronounce these things evil? All evil comes from man's darkened understanding, from his ignorance, from his false interpretation of life, and from his misuse of his subconscious mind. Uranium, lead, or some other metal could have been used as a medium of exchange. We use paper bills, checks, nickel, and silver surely these are not evil. Physicists and chemists know today that the only difference between one metal and another is the number and rate of motion of electrons revolving around a central nucleus. They can now change one metal into another through a bombardment of the atoms in the powerful cyclotron. Gold under certain conditions becomes mercury. I believe that our modern scientists in the near future will be able to make gold, silver, and other metals synthetically in the chemical laboratory. The cost may be prohibitive now, but it can be done. I cannot imagine any intelligent person seeing anything evil in electrons, neutrons, protons, and isotopes. The piece of paper in your pocket is composed of atoms and molecules with their electrons and protons arranged differently. Their number and rate of motion are different. That is the only way the paper differs from the silver in your pocket.

How to attract the money you need- Many years ago I met a young boy in Australia who wanted to become a physician and surgeon, but he had no money. I explained to him how a seed deposited in the soil attracts to itself everything necessary for its unfolding, and that all he had to do was to take a lesson from the seed and deposit the required idea in his subconscious mind. For expenses this young, brilliant boy used to clean out doctors' offices, wash windows, and do odd repair jobs. He told me that every night, as he went to sleep, he used to picture in his mind's eye a medical diploma on a wall with his name on it in big, bold letters. He used to clean and shine the framed diplomas in the medical building where he worked. It was not hard for him to engrave the image of a diploma in his mind and develop it there. Definite results followed as he persisted with his mental picture every night for about four months. The sequel of this story was very interesting. One of the doctors took a great liking to this young boy and after training him in the art of sterilizing instruments, giving hypodermic injections, and other miscellaneous first-aid work, he employed him as a technical assistant in his office. The doctor later sent him to medical school at his own expense. Today, this young man is a prominent medical doctor in Montreal, Canada. He discovered the law of attraction by using his subconscious mind the right way. He operated an age-old law, which says, "Having seen the end, you have willed the means to the realization of the end." The end in this case was to become a medical doctor. This young man was able to imagine, see, and feel the reality of being a doctor. He lived with that idea, sustained it, nourished it, and loved it until through his imagination it penetrated the layers of his subconscious mind and became a conviction, thereby attracting to him everything necessary for the fulfillment of his dream.

Why some men do not get a raise in pay- If you are working in a large organization and you are silently thinking of and resenting the fact you are underpaid, that you are not appreciated, and that you deserve more money and greater recognition, you are subconsciously severing your ties with that organization. You are setting a law in motion, and the superintendent or manager will say to you, "We have to let you go." Actually, you dismissed yourself. The manager was simply the instrument through which your own negative mental state was confirmed. It was an example of the law of action and reaction. The action was your thought, and the reaction was the response of your subconscious mind.

Obstacles and impediments on the pathway to riches- I am sure you have heard men say, "That fellow has a racket." "He is a racketeer." "He is getting money dishonestly." "He is a faker." "I knew him when he had nothing." "He is a crook, a thief, and a swindler." If you analyze the man who talks like that, you discover he is usually in want or suffering from some financial or physical illness. Perhaps his former college friends went up the ladder of success and excelled him. Now he is bitter and envious of their progress. In many instances this is the cause of his downfall. Thinking negatively of these classmates and condemning their wealth causes the wealth and prosperity he is praying for to vanish and flee away. He is condemning the thing he is praying for. He is praying two ways. On the one hand he is saying, "Wealth is flowing to me now," and in the next breath, silently or audibly, he is saying, "I resent that fellow's wealth." Always make it a special point to rejoice in the wealth of the other person.

Protect your investments- If you are seeking wisdom regarding investments, or if you are worried about your stocks or bonds, quietly claim, "Infinite intelligence governs and watches over all my financial transactions, and whatsoever I do shall prosper." Do this frequently and you will find that your investments will be wise; moreover, you will be protected from loss, as you will be prompted to sell your securities or holdings before any loss accrues to you.

You cannot get something for nothing- In large stores the management employs store detectives to prevent people from stealing. They catch a number of people every day trying to get something for nothing. All such people are living in the mental atmosphere of lack and limitation and are stealing from themselves peace, harmony, faith, honesty, integrity, good will, and confidence. Furthermore, they are attracting to themselves all manner of loss, such as, loss of character, prestige, social status, and peace of mind. These people lack faith in the source of supply and the understanding of how their minds work. If they would mentally call on the powers of their subconscious mind and claim that they are guided to their true expression, they would find work and constant supply. Then by honesty, integrity, and perseverance, they would become a credit to themselves and to society at large.

Your constant supply of money- Recognizing the powers of your subconscious mind and the creative power of your thought or mental image is the way to opulence, freedom, and constant supply. Accept the abundant life in your own mind. Your mental acceptance and expectancy of wealth has its own mathematics and mechanics of expression. As you enter into the mood of opulence, all things necessary for the abundant life will come to pass. Let this be your daily affirmation; write it in your heart, "I am one with the infinite riches of my subconscious mind. It is my right to be rich, happy, and successful. Money flows to me freely, copiously, and endlessly. I am forever conscious of my true worth. I give of my talents freely, and I am wonderfully blessed financially. It is wonderful!"

Step up this way to riches

1. Be bold enough to claim that it is your right to be rich and your deeper mind will honor your claim.

2. You don't want just enough to go around. You want all the money you need to do all the things you want to do and when you want to do them. Get acquainted with the riches of your

subconscious mind.

3.   When money is circulating freely in your life, you are economically healthy. Look at money like the tide and you will always have plenty of it. The ebb and flow of the tide is constant. When the tide is out, you are absolutely sure that it will return

4.   Knowing the laws of your subconscious mind, you will always be supplied regardless of what form money takes.

5.   One reason many people simply make ends meet and never have enough money is that they condemn money. What you condemn takes wings and

flies away.

6.   Do not make a god of money. It is only a symbol. Remember that the real riches are in your mind. You are here to lead a balanced life—this includes acquiring all the money you need.

7.   Don't make money your sole aim. Claim wealth, happiness, peace, true expression, and love, and personally radiate love and good will to all. Then your subconscious mind will give you compound interest in all these fields of expression.

8.   There is no virtue in poverty. It is a disease of the mind, and you should heal yourself of this mental conflict or

malady at once.

9.   You are not here to live in a hovel, to dress in rags, or to go hungry. You are here to lead the life more abundant.

10.   Never use the terms "filthy lucre" or "I despise money." You lose what you criticize. There is nothing good or bad, but thinking of it in either light makes it so.

11.   Repeat frequently, "I like money. I use it wisely, constructively, and judiciously. I release it with joy, and it returns a thousand fold."

12.   Money is not evil any more so than copper, lead, tin, or iron which you may find in the ground. All evil is due to

ignorance and misuse of the mind's powers.

13. To picture the end result in your mind causes your subconscious to respond and fulfill your mental picture.

14. Stop trying to get something for nothing. There is no such thing as a free lunch. You must give to receive. You must give mental attention to your goals, ideals, and enterprises, and your deeper mind will back you up. The key to wealth is application of the laws of the subconscious mind by impregnating it with the idea of wealth.

Henry Harrison Brown

Harmony There is neither health nor prosperity without harmony. There is no peace, no health, where there is want, be it want of material Supply, wisdom Supply or love Supply. Love, Truth and Dollars - these are necessary to human well-being. Mind, body and estate must be cared for. In order that there may be health, happiness and prosperity, there must be Harmony. This harmony is found in merely giving Self, the Soul, its way. Harmony is living in obedience to mental law. It is found in right thinking. Bane of Poverty Poverty is the main cause of the unrest, the dis-ease (the un-ease) that afflicts mankind. Remove poverty by right thinking and all attendant evils will disappear. This right thinking means that there shall be on the part of the individual a change of attitude toward the Dollar. Mental Attitude The prevalent attitude is want for the Dollar, belief that Dollars are power. This must be outgrown and the attitude must be that ALL POWER IS IN MAN. Dollars are machines with power delegated to them by man. They are useless without man. Dollars want me! is to be the thought of the "Coming man."

A few so think now and have obtained mastery of Supply. Demand and Supply It is a legitimate demand on the part of each individual that he have enough. To supply human needs is the function of the universe. All is for man. The sun shines for him; the waters run for him; the flowers bloom for him; the grain ripens for him; and the earth teems with beauty for him. All would be useless, would be purposeless, but for him. When he ceases to be, there is no use for the universe or anything in it. Without Man these are virtually non-existent. Man alone gives a meaning, a use, a value, a purpose to the universe. There is enough in the Universal One from which all things materialize, for each one to have enough to meet all desires without robbing any. Infinite Supply is all about us and yet there is want. Whose the fault?

Not of The One. It is in ourselves. We have not known how to claim, nor have we claimed our own. Law of Supply The Law is simple and it is laid down by the greatest political economist as well as the greatest Mental Scientist the world has in its historic records. He was not a theologian, neither did he deal with questions of a future life, as many seem to think; he was a sociologist and a socialist. He dealt with questions of "the life that now is."His name was Jesus.

He gave the Law thus: "Seek first the Kingdom of God and his righteousness. and all things shall be added unto you."

Analyze this: "Kingdom of God?" Where? "Within you." "God is Spirit," he said. "The Kingdom of God'" is then in the Soul. It is the Ego or Soul of man. Know thyself as Soul; know thyself as Spirit - this is the Law. Live rightly, is the meaning of "his righteousness."

Live in accord with your sense of right : obey your own conscience. Then all things shall be yours. Things of whatever kind, of all kinds, are manifestations of the One Substance. Things are, like yourself, manifestations of the One God. Dollars are things. Dollars are manifestations of the One God.

Plain directions, these: Live true to self; live spiritually; give the first place in your thought to the eternal, from which things come and then all things will come to you at need. "First?" Yes! Not things first, but that mental condition which controls things. Not Dollars first, but that mental attitude which attracts Dollars.

I Trust Myself That mental condition is Faith in Self as a manifestation of

Omnipotence, Faith in Self as a manifestation of the All-Good, Faith in the Universe as Justice, Faith in the Universal One as entirely Good, Faith in the Life yon are, to draw its necessary Supply of things demanded for its highest expression. Then let things come. This is all, but it is God. This is the "strait gate." Few there be that enter in, but all may.

You will then be the Master and things will take their right place. Become "one with God" by recognizing Him as King in your Soul. Listen to Him in the edicts of your Soul. Say, as you thus become negative to the Higher in you, "Now,

God, do your work your way, and it will be done satisfactorily to me." No one can fail when he assumes this attitude of Love and Trust. It would be an impotent God, and therefore no-God, that did not work when these conditions are made.

Poverty is a mental condition. It can be cured only by the Affirmation of Power to cure: I am part of the One and, in the One, possess all. I possess all! Affirm this and patiently wait for the manifestation. You have sown the thought-seed, now, like the rancher, wait for the sprouting and the harvest It can never fail you when, like him, you trust.

Cure of Poverty: Repeat this

Affirmation, no matter what the appearances. No matter if hungry, homeless and alone, affirm: - God is my Supply. My Supply is Infinite. Dollars want me!

Trust implicitly in the inviolable Law of Cause and Effect. You are Cause; Supply is the Effect that must follow your Affirmation.

In the past, you have sown poverty seeds, and are now reaping the crop. You do not enjoy this harvest. Sow, amid these results of previous sowing, Plenty-seeds and Plenty will come. Supply is yours when you sow Supply seeds. Sow, no matter how seemingly black the conditions. The seeds have God-in them and cannot fail.

Affirmations for Use: My SUPPLY IS INFINITE! For God is my Supply.

Supply can never fail me. Make this your Affirmation and hold it. HOLD IT.

Supply is Sure The Law of Supply is as sure as gravity. In this Affirmation, All is Mine! Dollars want me,! you have repolarized your aura. You have changed your vibrations and you will draw, as the magnet draws the needle, all you can use. Try it! Never let go of your trust that Dollars, or that for which they stand, will come. Thy Kingdom, O Soul, has come and thy will is done for God and Soul are One. "All is mine; 'tis but by asking: Ere I make my silent plea Life unlocks her richest treasures For my waiting eyes to see.

OPULENCE

You conquer fate by thought. If you think the fatal thought of men and institutions, you need never pull the trigger. The consequences of thinking inevitably follow. - Carlyle.

The Dollars Side: Personal ideals, of necessity, must differ, yet, since money represents objective power, its consideration must enter as a factor into every ideal of success. Money represents Supply. It stands in our thought, for food, clothing and shelter; for books, pictures and companionship; for enjoyment, unfoldment and expression. Material Supply is a necessity of Life. The Dollar is the concrete representative of this necessity. But the Dollar also means opportunity for the realization of high ideals.

The individual must be free and, until the necessities of life are assured, he is not free.

Personal Liberty: THUS THE DOLLAR STANDS FOR INDIVIDUAL LIBERTY. Personal liberty finds its basis in pecuniary independence. Financial independence and personal liberty bear very largely the relation of cause and effect. We can almost say that in the popular mind the Dollar confers liberty. In Soul Culture, a mental attitude of superiority to the Dollar results in personal liberty. There is no liberty to him who feels himself limited by the want of the Dollar.

Debt is one of the most tyrannical of masters. Mackay well says: "The debtor is ever a shame-faced dog, With his creditor's name on his collar."

There can be no liberty to him who feels the slavery of debt.

What is Success: SUCCESS LIES IN THE MENTAL ATTITUDE THAT

ARISES FROM THAT SENSE OF PERSONAL POWER WHICH MEETS EVERY CONDITION WITHOUT ANXIETY.

That cannot be called success which results in ill health and unhappiness, unrest or fear. Eliminate these from your ideal and you have, as a necessary concomitant of success, financial ease.

The New Thought: In the old competitive thought men sought business and wanted the dollar. Under the New Thought, it is: "Seek first the kingdom of God and its right living and all things necessary to my happiness will be added to me." The Soul has only to exercise its drawing power. When the conscious mind lets itself be led or drawn, it will be drawn to what it desires. Desire is the magnet. Let it have its way. Trust in your own Love of Truth and Love of Goodness and never question. That you desire it, is enough. That you desire it, is evidence that it already exists for you on the Soul-side. Be passive to the desire and LET it manifest. This attitude is itself Success.

What to Think Think positively: THINGS BELONG TO ME. I AM ALREADY POSSESSOR. They will come to me at NEED. Then LET them come. If they do not readily come, hold no anxious thought about them. Having accepted Truth that all is mine and that all DESIRED CONDITIONS OR THINGS WILL manifest, - keep on working in an equable, confident frame of mind, and LET them come. Anxiety, doubt, mistrust show that you have not claimed them as realities but have held them as dreams or possibilities. Until you hold them as realities, they cannot come.

The Right Mental Attitude: Change your attitude toward business. Do not seek it. See IT mentally already yours and LET it come. Attend yourself to details as they come to the surface.

Consider business a Principle that will run, as runs a mountain stream, when you remove your conscious will from it. All your concern is to be ready to use this business stream as the ranchman uses the water as it comes to his ditch.

There is but one Power and that is the Universal, the Infinite Power.

Business is Power: Business is a manifestation of the One Power. Use Power as does the telegrapher: LET it come and then direct it. The wisdom for the day comes with the day. LET it come by having faith in Self. Work each moment as if what you desire were here and it IS here.

Place of Money: As to money, regard it also as merely the power that keeps business going. Welcome its coming and rejoice at its going. It never does its work until, like water in the stream, it has passed under the wheel. The hoarded Dollar does not work and is of no real value to you. The Dollar you spend is the only one you really have, for by the experience of spending it you gain a growth, an enlargement, that is yours forever.

You are Power: Money is only delegated Power. You direct its expression. Change your attitude toward money. It is not "the almighty dollar."

Almighty Power uses the dollar. Say to the dollar, "I do not need you. You need me. You are of no use until my brain and hand use you. You wish to be used. You come to me that you may be used. I do not need a dollar. Dollars need me." Assume this mental attitude and see what a change it makes for you. When you have changed your aura, dollars will be drawn. You need not think of their coming, for they will come to you through the opportunities which this new mental attitude will reveal to you. Think only of using them.

Mental Attitude towards Dollars: Change your attitude towards the dollars you have. Tell them they are of no use until they are expended. As you see them lying about, say to them: "Idle dollars, go to work. Go out and circulate. Each one of you go and pay a million in wages and debts. When I need you, come back again. You are useless and have no value until you go to work." Then LET them go to work, knowing that, when you send this thought with them, they or their fellows will come back to you to be set at work.

Spend the Dollars: Before you spend a dollar, the question comes. "Is it right?" Whether you have a single dollar, or whether behind the one you think of spending are a million, makes no difference. If it is right to spend the dollar in the proposed way, had you the million, it is right thus to spend this, the lone one. Therefore, when you feel it is right to spend a dollar for any purpose, spend it as royally as if you were a millionaire. From the Inner Life, this message was given to me years ago: "Let a thought of use stand guard over your purse and then spend freely." Amend this by affirming: "A thought of the righteousness of the spending stands guard over my dollars and I send them forth with blessing."

Thoughts do the Work: These dollars, like every thought of good you send out, will return to bless. You do business with thoughts only; dollars are but materialized thoughts. Each dollar in any man's hand represents his thought in material form. Send out at all times with your dollars the thoughts you wish to return to you, for what you sow in your dollars, you reap in dollars that either do, or do not, come back to you. Put the thought of Success, Happiness and Health into every dollar that passes out and it will return so laden.

Poles of Thought: Having acquired the proper mental attitude, there is something necessary for you to do to draw the Dollar. Your magnet of desire must have two poles. First, you must have something which the world needs and is willing to pay for. In this respect you must follow the law of supply and demand. You must honestly feel that you will give the Dollar's worth for every Dollar that you desire. Secondly, you must, in all sincerity, dedicate every Dollar that comes to you to noble service. You can then feel that Dollars want you; that through them you can give what you have of value to the world. Feel that Dollars wish you to use them for the accomplishment of your purpose to use them justly. With this ideal, you can conscientiously invite Dollars and they will come. They need your heart, brain and hand that they may benefit the world.

What are Dollars? Dollars are manifestations of the One Infinite Substance as you are, but, unlike you, they are not Self Conscious. They have no power till you give them power. Make them feel this through your thought vibrations as you feel the importance of your work. They will then come to you to be used. They will not come, nor can you in this Thought draw them, to be hoarded. Use, Helpfulness and Happiness must be in your thought of Success. This held firmly, perseveringly, as your Affirmation, will turn the current of Dollars your way.

What to Think: Your thought should be: I possess that which the world wants. Dollars want me to use them in scattering that which I have to bless. Use these Affirmations persistently: Dollars Love me. Dollars Want me. I am ready to use dollars and they only come to me to be used. Make no limit as to the amount. Claim abundance. Claim all you can use for good, all that is needed to enable you to be useful and happy. Abundant Supply, be your demand.

Florence Scovel Shinn

One of the greatest messages given to the human race is that God is man's supply and that man can release, through his spoken word, all that belongs to him by divine right. He must, however, have perfect faith in his spoken word. Isaiah said, "My word shall not return unto me void, but shall accomplish that where it is sent." We know now, that words and thoughts are a tremendous vibratory force, ever moulding man's body and affairs.

A woman came to me in great distress and said she was to be sued on the fifteenth of the month for three thousand dollars. She knew no way of getting the money and was in despair. I told her God was her supply, and that there is a supply for every demand. So I spoke the word! I gave thanks that the woman would receive three thousand dollars at the right time in the right way. I told her she must have perfect faith, and act her perfect faith. The fifteenth came but no money had materialized. She called me on the 'phone and asked what she was to do.

I replied, "It is Saturday, so they won't sue you today, Your part is to act rich, thereby showing perfect faith that you will receive it by Monday." She asked me to lunch with her to keep up her courage. When I joined her at a restaurant, I said, "This is no time to economize. Order an expensive luncheon, act as if you have already received the three thousand dollars."

"All things whatsoever ye ask in prayer, believing, ye shall receive." "You must act as if you had already received." The next morning she called me on the 'phone and asked me to stay with her during the day, I said "No, you are divinely protected and God is never too late." In the evening she 'phoned again, greatly excited and said, "My dear, a miracle has happened! I was sitting in my room this morning, when the doorbell rang, I said to the maid: 'Don't let anyone in.' The maid however, looked out the window and said, 'It's your cousin with the long white beard.'

So I said, 'Call him back. I would like to see him.' He was just turning the corner, when he heard the maid's voice, and he came back. He talked for about an hour, and just as he was leaving he said, 'Oh, by the way, how are finances?'

I told him I needed the money, and he said, 'Why, my dear, I will give you three thousand dollars the first of the month. I didn't like to tell him I was going to be sued. What shall I do? I won't receive it till the first of the month, and I must have it tomorrow." I said, "I'll keep on 'treating.'"

I said, "Spirit is never too late. I give thanks she has received the money on the invisible plane and that it manifests on time." The next morning her cousin called her up and said, "Come to my office this morning and I will give you the money." That afternoon, she had three thousand dollars to her credit in the bank, and wrote checks as rapidly as her excitement would permit.

If one asks for success and prepares for failure, he will get the situation he has prepared for. For example: A man came to me asking me to speak the word that a certain debt would be wiped out.

I found he spent his time planning what he would say to the man when he did not pay his bill, thereby neutralizing my words. He should have seen himself paying the debt.

We have a wonderful illustration of this in the bible, relating to the three kings who were in the desert, without water for their men and horses. They consulted the prophet Elisha, who gave them this astonishing message:

"Thus saith the Lord - Ye shall not see wind, neither shall ye see rain, yet make this valley full of ditches." Man must prepare for the thing he has asked for, when there isn't the slightest sign of it in sight. For example: A woman found it necessary to look for an apartment during the year when there was a great shortage of apartments in New York. It was considered almost an impossibility, and her friends were sorry for her and said, "Isn't it too bad, you'll have to store your furniture and live in a hotel." She replied, "You needn't feel sorry for me, I'm a superman, and I'll get an apartment."

She spoke the words: "Infinite Spirit, open the way for the right apartment."

She knew there was a supply for every demand, and that she was "unconditioned," working on the spiritual plane, and that "one with God is a majority."

She had contemplated buying new blankets, when the "tempter," the adverse thought or reasoning mind, suggested, "Don't buy the blankets, perhaps, after all, you won't get an apartment and you will have no use for them."

She promptly replied (to herself): "I'll dig my ditches by buying the blankets!" So she prepared for the apartment - acted as though she already had it.

She found one in a miraculous way, and it was given to her although there were over two hundred other applicants. The blankets showed active faith. It is needless to say that the ditches dug by the three kings in the desert were filled to over-flowing. (Read, II Kings) Getting into the spiritual swing of things is no easy matter for the average person. The adverse thoughts of doubt and fear surge from the subconscious. They are the "army of the aliens" which must be put to flight. This explains why it is so often, "darkest before the dawn." A big demonstration is usually preceded by tormenting thoughts.

Having made a statement of high spiritual truth one challenges the old beliefs in the subconscious, and "error is exposed" to be put out. This is the time when one must make his affirmations of truth repeatedly, and rejoice and give thanks that he has already received, "Before ye call I shall answer." This means that "every good and perfect gift" is already man's awaiting his recognition. Man can only receive what he sees himself receiving. The children of Israel were told that they could have all the land they could see.

This is true of every man. He has only the land within his own mental vision.

Every great work, every big accomplishment, has been brought into manifestation through holding to the vision, and often just before the big achievement, comes apparent failure and discouragement. The children of Israel when they reached the "Promised Land," were afraid to go in, for they said it was filled with giants who made them feel like grasshoppers.

"And there we saw the giants and we were in our own sight as grasshoppers." This is almost every man's experience. However, the one who knows spiritual law, is undisturbed by appearance, and rejoices while he is "yet in captivity."

That is, he holds to his vision and gives thanks that the end is accomplished, he has received. Jesus Christ gave a wonderful example of this.

He said to his disciples: "Say not ye, there are yet four months and then cometh the harvest? Behold, I say unto you, lift up your eyes and look on the fields; for they are ripe already to harvest." His clear vision pierced the "world of matter" and he saw clearly the fourth dimensional world, things as they really are, perfect and complete in Divine Mind. So man must ever hold the vision of his journey's end and demand the manifestation of that which he has already received. It may be his perfect, health, love, supply, self-expression, home or friends. They are all finished and perfect ideas registered in Divine Mind (man's own superconscious mind) and must come through him, not to him.

For example: A man came to me asking for treatments for success. It was imperative that he raise, within a certain, fifty-thousand dollars for his business. The time limit was almost up, when he came to me in despair. No one wanted to invest in his enterprise, and the bank had flatly refused a loan.

I replied: "I suppose you lost your temper while at the bank, therefore your power. You can control any situation if you first control yourself." "Go back to the bank," I added, "and I will treat."

My treatment was: "You are identified in love with the spirit of everyone connected with the bank. Let the divine idea come out of this situation." He replied, "Woman, you are talking about an impossibility.

Tomorrow is Saturday; the bank closes at twelve, and my train won't get me there until ten, and the time limit is up tomorrow, and anyway they won't do it. It's too late." I replied, "God doesn't need any time and is never too late. With Him all things are possible." I added, "I don't know anything about business, but I know all about God."

He replied: "It all sounds fine when I sit here listening to you, but when I go out it's terrible." He lived in a distant city, and I did not hear from him for a week, then came a letter.

It read: "You were right. I raised the money, and will never again doubt the truth of all that you told me."

I saw him a few weeks later, and I said, "what happened? You evidently had plenty of time, after all." He replied, "My train was late, and I got there just fifteen minutes to twelve. I walked into the bank quietly and said, 'I have come for the loan,' and they gave it to me without a question."

It was the last fifteen minutes of the time allotted to him, and Infinite Spirit was not too late. In this instance the man could never have demonstrated alone. He needed someone to help him hold to the vision. This is what one man can do for another.

Jesus Christ knew the truth of this when he said: "If two of you shall agree on earth as touching anything that they shall ask, it shall be done for them of my Father which is in heaven." One gets too close to his own affairs and becomes doubtful and fearful. The friend or "healer" sees clearly the success, health, or prosperity, and never wavers, because he is not close to the situation. It is much easier to "demonstrate" for someone else than for one's self, so a person should not hesitate to ask for help, if he feels himself wavering. A keen observer of life once said, "no man can fail, if some one person sees him successful." Such is the power of the vision, and many a great man owed his success to a wife, or sister, or a friend who "believed in him" and held without wavering to the perfect pattern!

The way of abundance is a one-way

street.

As the old saying is, "there are no two ways about it." You are either heading for lack, or heading for abundance. The man with a rich consciousness and the man with a poor consciousness are not walking on the same mental street.

There is a lavish supply, divinely planned for each individual.

The rich man is tapping it, for rich thoughts produce rich surroundings. Change your thoughts, and in the twinkling of an eye, all your conditions change. Your world is a world of crystallized ideas, crystallized words.

Sooner or later, you reap the fruits of your words and thoughts. "Words are bodies or forces which move spirally and return in due season to cross the lives of their creators." People who are always talking lack and limitation, reap lack and limitation.

You cannot enter the Kingdom of Abundance bemoaning (complaining) your lot. I know a woman who had always been limited in her ideas of prosperity. She was continually making her old clothes "do," instead of buying new clothes. She was very careful of what money she had, and was always advising her husband not to spend so much. She said repeatedly, "I don't want anything I can't afford." She couldn't afford much, so she didn't have much. Suddenly her whole world cracked up. Her husband left her, weary of her nagging and limited thoughts. She was in despair, when one day she came across a book on metaphysics. It explained the power of thought and words.

She realized that she had invited every unhappy experience by wrong thinking. She laughed heartily at her mistakes, and decided to profit by them. She determined to prove the law of abundance. She used what money she had, fearlessly, to show her faith in her invisible supply. She relied upon God as the source of her prosperity. She no longer voiced lack and limitation. She kept herself feeling and looking prosperous.

Her old friends scarcely recognized her. She had swung into the way of abundance. More money came to her than she had ever had before. Unheard-

of doors opened - amazing channels

were freed. She became very successful
in a work she had had no training for.

She found herself on miracle ground.
What had happened? She had changed
the quality of her words and thoughts.
She had taken God into her confidence,
and into all her affairs. She had many
eleventh hour demonstrations, but her

supply always came, for she dug her ditches and gave thanks without wavering.

Someone called me up recently and said, "I am looking desperately for a position." I replied, "Don't look desperately for it, look for it with praise and thanksgiving, for Jesus Christ, the greatest of metaphysicians, said to pray with praise and thanksgiving."

Praise and thanksgiving open the gates, for expectancy always wins. Of course, the law is impersonal, and a dishonest person with rich thoughts will attract riches - but, "a thing ill-got has ever bad

success," as Shakespeare says. It will be of short duration and will not bring happiness.

We have only to read the papers to see that the way of the transgressor is hard. That is the reason it is so necessary to make your demands aright on the Universal Supply, and ask for what is yours by divine right and under grace in a perfect way.

Some people attract prosperity, but cannot hold it. Sometimes their heads are turned, sometimes they lose it through fear and worry.

A friend in one of my question and answer classes told this story. Some people in his home town, who had always been poor, suddenly struck oil in their backyard. It brought great riches. The father joined the country club and went in for golf. He was no longer

young - the exercise was too much for

him and he dropped dead on the links. This filled the whole family with fear. They all decided they might have heart trouble, so they are now in bed with trained nurses watching every heartbeat.

In the race-thought people must worry

about something.

They no longer worried about money, so they shifted their worries to health. The old idea was, "that you can't have everything." If you got one thing, you'd lose another. People were always saying, "Your luck won't last," "It's too good to be true." Jesus Christ said, "In the world (world thought) there is tribulation, but be of good cheer, I have overcome the world (thought)."

In the superconscious, there is a lavish supply for every demand, and your good is perfect and permanent. "If thou return to the Almighty, thou shalt be built up (in consciousness), thou shalt put away iniquity far from thy tabernacles."

"Then shalt thou lay up gold as dust, the gold of Ophir as the stones of the brooks."

"Yea, the Almighty shall be thy defense and thou shalt have plenty of silver." What a picture of opulence! The result of "Returning to the Almighty (in consciousness)." With the average person (who has thought in terms of lack for a long time) it is very difficult to build up a rich consciousness.

I have a student who has attracted great success by making the statement: "I am the daughter of the King! My rich Father now pours out his abundance upon me. I am the daughter of the King! Everything makes way for me."

Many people put up with limited conditions because they are too lazy (mentally), to think themselves out of them. You must have a great desire for financial freedom, you must feel yourself rich, you must see yourself rich, you must continually prepare for riches. Become as a little child and make believe you are rich. You are then impressing the subconscious with expectancy. The imagination is man's workshop, the scissors of the mind, where he is constantly cutting out the events of his life!

The superconscious is the realm of inspiration, revelation, illumination and intuition. Intuition is usually known as a hunch. I do not apologize for the word "hunch" anymore. It is now in Webster's latest dictionary.

I had a hunch to look up "hunch," and there it was. The superconscious is the realm of perfect ideas. The great genius captures his thoughts from the superconscious.

"Without the vision (imagination) my people perish."

When people have lost the power to image their good, they "perish" (or go under).

Trust in the source of your supply: A priest went to visit a nunnery in France, where they fed many children. One of the nuns, in despair, told the priest they had no food, the children must go hungry. She said that they had but one piece of silver (about the value of a quarter of a dollar). They needed food and clothing.

The priest said, "Give me the coin."

She handed it to him and he threw it out the window.

"Now," he said, "rely entirely upon God."

Within a short time friends arrived with plenty of food and gifts of money. This doesn't mean to throw away what money you have, but don't depend upon it. Depend upon your invisible supply, the Bank of the Imagination.   Let us now attach ourselves to God and have peace. For He shall be our gold, our silver and our riches.

The inspiration of the Almighty shall be my defense and I shall have plenty of silver.

Man comes into the world financed by God, with all that he desires or requires already on his pathway. This supply is released through faith and the Spoken Word. "If thou canst believe, all things are possible."

For example: A woman came to me one day to tell me of her experience in using an affirmation she had read in my book, "The Game of Life and How to Play It." She was without experience but desired a good position on the stage.

She took the affirmation: "Infinite Spirit, open the way for my great abundance. I am an irresistible magnet for all that belongs to me by Divine Right." She was given a very important part in a successful opera.

She said: "It was a miracle, due to the affirmation, which I repeated hundreds of times, it really works!"

I hope you enjoyed this timeless knowledge. This information was exactly what I used to create my multiple 6 figure income, and you can use it too. Remember, if you have knowledge but don't use that knowledge, YOU DON'T REALLY HAVE KNOWLEDGE! Use this stuff, it really works!

Here is a list of Wealth Affirmations that should be repeated often with conviction and authority (To train the Subconscious Mind):

Every day in every way, my wealth is increasing!

I deserve prosperity, and I accept prosperity in my life!

I see and construct prosperity easily and effortlessly!

I will visualize myself open and receptive to all wealth!

I was destined to be prosperous. I have abundance to share and to spare!

Excerpts of the book titles used:

"The Science of Getting Rich", By Wallace D. Wattles

"The Power of Your Subconscious Mind", By Joseph Murphy

"Dollars Want Me", By Henry Harrison Brown

"The Game Of life and How To Play It"- By Florence Scovel Shinn

153